JONAH

You Can't Outrun Grace

Street Level Christianity SERIES

PAUL TRIPP

© Copyright 2017 by The Hub

All rights reserved.

Any reproduction of this material in any form
without written permission of the publisher is strictly prohibited.

Unless otherwise indicated, Scripture quotations are from
The Holy Bible, English Standard Version, ®
Copyright © 2001 by Crossway, a publishing ministry
of Good News Publishers.
Used by permission. All rights reserved.

1st edition 2017

Published by

THE HUB

PO BOX 551792
Dallas, TX 75355-1792

Printed in the United States

THE HUB | GOTOTHEHUB.COM

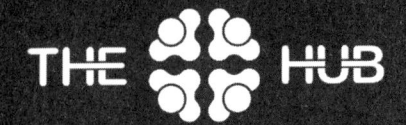

STRENGTHEN YOUR COMMUNITY WITH THE
LARGEST ON-DEMAND
VIDEO BIBLE STUDY LIBRARY!

FRANCIS CHAN   JENNIE ALLEN   MATT CHANDLER   TIM KELLER

over 70 dynamic speakers to choose from

RENT. BUY. PRINT STUDY GUIDES. ON DEMAND.

GOTOTHEHUB.COM

TABLE OF CONTENTS

	PAGE
ACKNOWLEDGEMENTS	VI
STUDY TIPS	VII
ABOUT THE AUTHOR	VIII

ONE	What controls your heart?	1
TWO	Do you have God's heart?	5
THREE	Do you know God's uncomfortable grace?	9
FOUR	Has God's grace changed you?	15
FIVE	What is your potential?	19
SIX	What does God's love look like?	23
SEVEN	Do you want what God wants?	27
EIGHT	What does it mean to follow God?	31

ACKNOWLEDGEMENTS

Thank you to Paul Tripp for his incredible teaching and wisdom of God's Word. We are inspired by his passion to communicate hope in God's restoration within a broken world.

Ben Fallon and Steve Sarkisian, we are grateful for all your hard work and friendship in this process.

We could never have accomplished this curriculum without the help of:

Kyle McCarthy
Drew Fitzgerald
Eleazar Ruiz
Shatrine Krake / Krake Designs
Puritan Coffee
The entire Hub Team

STUDY TIPS

BEFORE YOU GO ANY FURTHER...READ THIS!

Thank you for being willing to facilitate this study on Jonah. I believe that these 48 Old Testament verses summarize a biblical worldview, and God has chosen for you to help your brothers and sisters develop more accurate vision. How exciting!

As the facilitator, your role is both similar and different to those participating. You should pay close attention to the material and listen with a humble heart, because God wants to teach you things. At the same time, it's your role to lead others and be available to give counsel, advice and wisdom.

Here are some recommendations for you to keep in mind as you lead:

- **Watch all eight video lessons** and follow along with the Discussion Guide in advance of your first group gathering; having a full understanding of Jonah before this study begins will allow you to facilitate more effectively.
- **Agree on a start and end time** and honor it; eight, 60 to 75-minute gatherings should provide ample time to finish this study.
- **Facilitate each gathering,** asking questions and encouraging participation. Solicit answers from multiple participants; don't let the same person answer every question. For some questions, it might be appropriate to ask everyone, but don't force anyone to answer.
- **Allow time** for participants to answer, rephrasing the question when necessary. Avoid answering questions yourself; contribute, but don't dominate.
- **Affirm everyone's participation** and allow "questionable" responses to remain uncorrected. Rejecting answers, or allowing others to reject answers, can result in an environment of timidity and reduce honesty among participants. Often, a "questionable" or "faulty" answer will be corrected over the course of time.
- **Lead with transparency** and vulnerability, and others will follow. Remember, there's nothing that could ever be exposed about us that Jesus hasn't already covered. We have confidence to admit moral failure and cry out for help.
- **Adjust as necessary.** If you believe that skipping certain questions or spending an entire lesson on one question in particular will benefit your gathering, do so. There are multiple discussion questions for each lesson, and my assumption is that you won't be able to ask all of them in each lesson without rushing. This guide is merely a template, so select questions you believe are most relevant.

ABOUT THE
AUTHOR

Dr. Paul David Tripp is a pastor, author and conference speaker. He is the president of Paul Tripp Ministries and works to connect the transforming power of Jesus Christ to everyday life.

This vision has led Paul to write many books on Christian living and travel around the world speaking at events. Paul's driving passion is to help people understand how the gospel of Jesus Christ speaks with practical hope into all the things people experience in this broken world.

PT WEB **PaulTripp.com**
FACEBOOK **Facebook.com/PDTripp**
TWITTER **@PaulTripp**

ONE
What controls your heart?

Before we get into the book of Jonah, you need to understand what this story is about. In only forty-eight verses we will see four major themes:

1) At the center of the universe is a God of awesome, stunning, incalculable glory.
2) We live in an incredibly sinful, broken world.
3) We were designed to live for something greater than ourselves.
4) There is a beautiful reality of powerful transforming grace at work in the world.

Our diseased hearts tell us a different story. Sin tells us we are the center of the universe, that we don't need Jesus, and that our personal kingdoms are greater than God's eternal kingdom. Far too often we live as God-amnesiacs: we know the facts about God but live as if He doesn't exist. We live as if the most holy things in our lives are our wants, our feelings, and our needs. We are all controlled by something. **The question is: what controls you?**

> "We can be God-amnesiacs in our marriages, in our parenting, at our work, in our finances... we can forget that we don't live in the center of the world, God does."

1) If God is not dominating the center of your life, you will put yourself in His place. How have you lived as a God-amnesiac this week? Be specific.

_____
_____
_____
_____
_____

2) Read **2 Corinthians 5:14-15 (ESV):**

For the love of Christ controls us, because we have concluded this: that one has died for all, therefore all have died; and he died for all, that those who live might no longer live for themselves but for him who for their sake died and was raised.

How does the Word of God confront your God-amnesia? How could you have acted differently this past week?

_____
_____
_____
_____
_____

> "It's impossible for you to minimize sin without devaluing God's grace, because the only people who get excited about God's grace are people who get up every morning and name themselves as sinners."

3) It is tempting to minimize our sin rather than admitting how incredibly broken we are. How are you "a very skilled self-swindler" when it comes to your sin? Be specific.

_____
_____
_____
_____
_____
_____

4) The theology of the sinfulness of man is the one thing none of us believe. We prove this when we minimize our sins and become defensive when others point out our sins. Do you live in a way that shows you believe you are sinful? How, specifically?

_____
_____
_____
_____
_____
_____

5) When was the last time you got angry? Was it about God's kingdom or your own little kingdom? What really controls your emotions?

_____
_____
_____
_____
_____
_____

"I have one hope in life and death: it's the grace of God. It's forgiving, rescuing, transforming and ultimately delivering grace. Jonah preaches that grace from beginning to end."

STREET LEVEL TRUTH ::

There is a God who controls the universe, and you was meant to live for him and not for yourself. This world is broken by sin, and grace is your only hope. You need a Savior. Jonah's life is a huge neon sign pointing us to Jesus.

PRAYER ::

God, I confess I live for my own little kingdom far too often. I confess I live like your grace and commands are insignificant. I know I am called to live for something bigger than myself every day. Give me the strength and grace to live for your holy kingdom. I know my heart is diseased and my only hope is Jesus who has taken my sin and shame to the cross. Lord, I pray that truth alone will control my heart. Amen.

MEMORY VERSE ::

2 Corinthians 5:14-15 (ESV)

For the love of Christ controls us, because we have concluded this: that one has died for all, therefore all have died; and he died for all, that those who live might no longer live for themselves but for him who for their sake died and was raised.

TWO

Do you have God's heart?

In the last session, we saw how we are willing to minimize our sin and overlook our shortcomings. In the same way, we minimize our faith by rejecting the difficult call of God in favor of comfort. We evaluate our Christian lives by our church attendance and emotional worship but don't walk across the street to tell our neighbor about Jesus. How do you respond when God chooses an experience for you that you would never plan for yourself? Could it be that somewhere, somehow, in some way, you are running from God?

> Now the word of the Lord came to Jonah the son of Amittai, saying, "Arise, go to Nineveh, that great city, and call out against it, for their evil has come up before me." But Jonah rose to flee to Tarshish from the presence of the Lord. He went down to Joppa and found a ship going to Tarshish. So he paid the fare and went down into it, to go with them to Tarshish, away from the presence of the Lord. **Jonah 1:1-3 (ESV)**

"Let's not be too hard on Jonah. Jonah is in the Bible because he's like us."

1) We often ask God to show us his plan for our life, but then choose to reject that plan when it is difficult. How have you run from God's difficult plan this past week?

___

___

___

___

2) According to the video, why is it delusional to run from God? When was the last time you gave in to that delusion?

_____
_____
_____
_____
_____
_____

"If sin is less than sinful to you, you won't make the choices in life that God has designed you to make."

3) There are three reasons we run from God. The first is that **we do not share God's sensitivity to sin.** As a result, we neither confess our sins nor have compassion for the sinfulness of others. What practices do you need to adopt in order to fuel greater confession and compassion in your own life? Be specific.

_____
_____
_____
_____
_____
_____
_____
_____
_____

> "This book starts where all of us should start, with the question, 'Do I have the heart of God?' And my answer is: a little bit, but there's work to be done."

4) The second reason we run from God is that **we don't carry a practical commitment to God's plan.** We believe our plans stand above God's plans. What happens to your attitude and behavior when your plans can't be sovereign? Is there any sin you need to confess right now?

_____
_____
_____
_____
_____
_____

5) The last reason we run from God is that **we don't have a commitment to God's grace.** Are you desperate for His grace? List the ways God has shown you grace today.

_____
_____
_____
_____
_____
_____

STREET LEVEL TRUTH ::

Jesus took every ounce of your rejection so that in your moments of confession, no matter how dark, you would never again see the back of God's head. You can run to God even when you don't have His heart in the way you should. Even though we are prone to run from God, He will never turn His back on us because of what Jesus has done for us.

PRAYER ::

God, I'm in desperate need of help today. I pray that you would send your helpers my way. And Lord, please give me the humility to receive the help when it comes. Form in us a heart like your own so that, rather than running from your plan, we would love your plan. Rather than owning my life, I desire to live surrendered to You. Amen.

MEMORY VERSE ::

Psalm 51:10 (ESV)

Create in me a clean heart, O God, and renew a right spirit within me.

THREE

Do you know God's uncomfortable grace?

The story of Jonah puts two seemingly unrelated attributes of God's character together: anger and grace. As they intertwine in Jonah's story we see how both are necessary for our redemption. God is merciful, and he shows us his anger so that we can begin to surrender to the grace of the one who is our only hope. Grace is more than a tender touch of relief. Grace is uncomfortable.

But the Lord hurled a great wind on the sea, so that the ship threatened to break up. Then the mariners were afraid, and each cried out to his god. And they hurled the cargo that was in the ship into the sea to lighten it for them. But Jonah had gone down into the inner part of the ship and had lain down and was fast asleep. So the captain came and said to him, "What do you mean, you sleeper? Arise, call out to your god! Perhaps the god will give a thought to us, that we may not perish.

And they said to one another, "Come, let us cast lots, that we may know on whose account this evil has come upon us." So they cast lots, and the lot fell on Jonah. Then they said to him, "Tell us on whose account this evil has come upon us. What is your occupation? And where do you come from? What is your country? And of what people are you?" And he said to them, "I am a Hebrew, and I fear the Lord, the God of heaven, who made the sea and the dry land." Then the men were exceedingly afraid and said to him, "What is this that you have done!" For the men knew that he was fleeing from the presence of the Lord, because he had told them.

Then they said to him, "What shall we do to you, that the sea may quiet down for us?" For the sea grew more and more tempestuous. He said to them, "Pick me up and hurl me into the sea; then the sea will quiet down for you, for I know it is because of me that this great tempest has come upon you." Nevertheless, the men rowed hard to get back to dry land, but they could not, for the sea grew more and more tempestuous against them. Therefore they called out to the Lord, "O Lord, let us not perish for this man's life, and lay not on us innocent blood, for you, O Lord, have done as it pleased you." So they picked up Jonah and hurled him into the sea, and the sea ceased from its raging. Then the men feared the Lord exceedingly, and they offered a sacrifice to the Lord and made vows.

And the Lord appointed a great fish to swallow up Jonah. And Jonah was in the belly of the fish three days and three nights. **Jonah 1:4-17 (ESV)**

1) Does God's anger bother you? Why?

_____
_____
_____
_____
_____
_____

2) How is God's anger different than your anger? What is the purpose of God's anger?

_____
_____
_____
_____
_____
_____

> "A world without God's anger is utterly unlivable."

3) On the cross, the anger and grace of God come together. The anger of God rests on Christ so that we would be shown grace. Is God angry with your personal sin? How does God show you grace every day?

_____
_____
_____
_____
_____

> "Don't confuse theological knowledge and biblical literacy with spiritual maturity...You don't just think your theology; you live your theology."

4) How do God's holy anger and grace change your view of yourself and your view of others? How should this change the way you live? Be specific.

_____
_____
_____
_____
_____

5) Do difficulty and hardship in your life change your view of God? How do you try to "lighten the load" or cast blame?

___
___
___
___
___
___

"Helplessness is the doorway to hope."

6) God is gracious enough to make us uncomfortable. In hardship, he softens our hearts and shows us the futility of our own wisdom and strength. Have you encountered God's uncomfortable grace? List some practical ways that you can rely on His wisdom, strength, and righteousness more this week.

___
___
___
___
___
___
___
___
___
___

STREET LEVEL TRUTH ::

If you're not suffering now, you're near someone who is. If you're not suffering now, you will someday. One of the reasons you will suffer is because He loves you. He will use that difficulty to soften your heart and to bring you to the end of yourself, so that you put your faith in Him. Redemption is about the anger and grace of God coming together for our good, for our rescue, and for our forgiveness.

PRAYER ::

Lord, thank you for your redemption in Christ. We see the power of your anger in a storm that made seasoned sailors afraid. We see that anger is not meant for condemnation, or our judgment, but for our redemption. Thank you for Jesus, who willingly received the storm of your anger so that grace would flow to us. Thank you. In Jesus' name, amen.

MEMORY VERSE ::

2 Corinthians 12:9 (ESV)

But he said to me, "My grace is sufficient for you, for my power is made perfect in weakness." Therefore, I will boast all the more gladly of my weaknesses, so that the power of Christ may rest upon me.

THOUGHTS ::

FOUR

Has God's grace changed you?

The second chapter of Jonah allows us to overhear an intensely intimate prayer. God gives us a window into the belly of a fish swimming deep in the sea so that we can see how grace changes a person's heart. This change, or repentance, happens in three major moves:

1) Remembrance
2) Confession
3) Commitment

Then Jonah prayed to the Lord his God from the belly of the fish, saying, "I called out to the Lord, out of my distress, and he answered me; out of the belly of Sheol I cried, and you heard my voice. For you cast me into the deep, into the heart of the seas, and the flood surrounded me; all your waves and your billows passed over me. Then I said, 'I am driven away from your sight; yet I shall again look upon your holy temple.' The waters closed in over me to take my life; the deep surrounded me; weeds were wrapped about my head at the roots of the mountains. I went down to the land whose bars closed upon me forever; yet you brought up my life from the pit, O Lord my God. When my life was fainting away I remembered the Lord, and my prayer came to you into your holy temple. Those who pay regard to vain idols forsake their hope of steadfast love. But I with the voice of thanksgiving will sacrifice to you; what I have vowed I will pay. Salvation belongs to the Lord!"

And the Lord spoke to the fish, and it vomited Jonah out upon the dry land. **Jonah 2 (ESV)**

1) We often pray in abstract terms in order to avoid responsibility for our actions. Euphemistic prayer creates spiritual paralysis, because we excuse ourselves from confessing our sin. Is there distress in your life that you need to be honest about? If so, what is it?

_____
_____
_____
_____
_____

"Jonah didn't need more moral muscle or knowledge of the law. He needed grace because only grace can change the heart."

2) The first move of God's grace is **remembrance**. God caused Jonah to remember him by means of the grace of trouble. In what ways are you actively running from and trying to forget God? How is He causing you to remember Him?

_____
_____
_____
_____
_____

"Confession and repentance aren't an event; they're a process."

3) The second move of God's grace is **confession**. When we forget God we quickly put ourselves on His throne and worship our own wants, feelings, and desires. How have you turned from God? Be specific.

_____
_____
_____
_____
_____

4) The third move of God's grace is **commitment**. Grace changes us from runners to worshippers. Look at the ways you have run from God listed in questions 2 and 3. How is God changing those running habits into holy worship?

_____
_____
_____
_____
_____

"Your hope is never what's inside of your heart. Your hope is what's in God's heart."

5) If either law or your commitment to personal reformation could rescue you, Jesus would've never had to come. Because of Christ, we can receive the amazing grace of God which forgives us of our sin and changes our hearts.

_____
_____
_____
_____

STREET LEVEL TRUTH ::

If your commitment to personal reformation could rescue you, we would have no need for Christ. In fact, he would never have come to us. But he has come. He has come because we need Him. Because of Christ, we can receive the amazing grace of God which forgives our sinfulness and changes our hearts.

PRAYER ::

Lord, help me to abandon my euphemistic way of talking about my trouble. Cause me to remember you. Cause me to begin to confess, commit, and repent to you. I pray that you would change my heart like you changed the heart of Jonah. How sweet is your grace! Thank you for your grace. I confess it is my single hope. In Jesus' name, amen.

MEMORY VERSE ::

Psalm 42:5 (ESV)

Why are you cast down, O my soul, and why are you in turmoil within me? Hope in God; for I shall again praise him, my salvation and my God.

FIVE

What is your potential?

The story of Jonah helps us understand the scary call of God. When faced with the impossible, we typically question our ability to accomplish it. Can I do this? Am I able? But God never intends us to do the impossible alone or by our own efforts. God calls us to the impossible because He is able to accomplish it. In only five verses God shows us how to change the way we measure our potential.

> *Then the word of the LORD came to Jonah the second time, saying, "Arise, go to Nineveh, that great city, and call out against it the message that I tell you." So Jonah arose and went to Nineveh, according to the word of the LORD. Now Nineveh was an exceedingly great city, three days' journey in breadth. Jonah began to go into the city, going a day's journey. And he called out, "Yet forty days, and Nineveh shall be overthrown!" And the people of Nineveh believed God. They called for a fast and put on sackcloth, from the greatest of them to the least of them.* **Jonah 3:1-5 (ESV)**

"God has the power to do whatever he wants to do through whomever he calls to whomever he wants."

1) Like Jonah, we choose to run from God when he calls us to scary or impossible situations. Our obedience is based on our perceived potential. We believe we are unable to accomplish his call, and therefore are unwilling to try. Is your obedience based on your own potential? When are you most likely to run from God?

___

___

___

___

"There is no finality of human decision, behavior, or action that can't be turned around by the grace of Jesus."

2) You cannot be totally confident in your potential while knowing how sinful you truly are. If you were in God's place, how would you have judged Jonah? How would you judge someone like you?

___

___

___

___

3) God came to Jonah "a second time" with the same grace that God has shown us in Jesus Christ. Are your decisions based in the fear of God's judgment or in the grace that knows no boundaries?

___

___

___

___

4) God called Jonah out of his comfort zone to go to his enemies with an unpopular message. This call was not just scary, it was impossible! Is God calling you to do something scary or even impossible? Write it down. Do you want to run from this call?

_____
_____
_____
_____
_____

5) God's grace confronts our fears. Read Galatians 2:20. God's power is not limited by your abilities or by results. How does that truth confront your fears? Be specific.

_____
_____
_____
_____
_____

6) God's grace comforts our hearts. Read Galatians 2:20 again. God's love for you is not based on your abilities or results. How does the power of Christ in you comfort your fears and give you peace in your anxieties? Be specific.

_____
_____
_____
_____
_____

"God does not call us because we are able, he calls us because he is able."

STREET LEVEL TRUTH ::

Your call is not to be the agent of change, but a tool in hands of the One who changes hearts. The measure of your potential is your savior. Surrendering to God allows very ordinary people to do extraordinary, restorative things.

PRAYER ::

God, thank you for Jesus. Help me learn that my potential is not based on my abilities, but on the completed work of Christ. Help me remember that even when your call appears impossible, you are able. My potential is rooted in you. Lord, may I respond to you daily in courage and joy through the power of Christ in me. I praise and thank you. Amen.

MEMORY VERSE ::

Galatians 2:20 (ESV)

I have been crucified with Christ. It is no longer I who live, but Christ who lives in me. And the life I now live in the flesh I live by faith in the Son of God, who loved me and gave himself for me.

SIX

What does God's love look like?

We serve a sovereign God who controls every detail of the universe. He is also a God who hears our cries and is willing to forgive. Because of this, we know that even His harsh words are intended for our good. No matter how much we've messed up, there is a God who gives us a hard word and a tender heart.

> The word reached the king of Nineveh, and he arose from his throne, removed his robe, covered himself with sackcloth, and sat in ashes. And he issued a proclamation and published through Nineveh, "By the decree of the king and his nobles: Let neither man nor beast, herd nor flock, taste anything. Let them not feed or drink water, but let man and beast be covered with sackcloth, and let them call out mightily to God. Let everyone turn from his evil way and from the violence that is in his hands. Who knows? God may turn and relent and turn from his fierce anger, so that we may not perish."
>
> When God saw what they did, how they turned from their evil way, God relented of the disaster that he had said he would do to them, and he did not do it.
> *Jonah 3:6-10 (ESV)*

"Jonah presents to us an unshakably sovereign God who is unchangeable, who repents. And you need to put that in your theological pipe and smoke it."

1) We are all sinners. That means that our relationships are broken and hurt by sin. Overlooking that damage is not loving. How does speaking difficult truth expose sin and strengthen relationships?

2) God has lovingly pronounced judgment on us because of our sin. (See Romans 6:23.) Do you believe your personal sin should be judged? How does your sin damage your relationship with God?

3) God's judgment is intended to bring us to repentance. What does this teach you about his character? What does this tell you about his love for you?

"If you announce judgment, it's not because you intend to judge; it is because you intend to redeem."

4) It should amaze us that God hears and responds to our prayers. How should your prayer life change in light of this truth? Be specific.

___
___
___
___
___

5) God gave Jonah a message of judgment intended to save a great city. God has given you the message of Jesus Christ intended to save the world. How does the story of Jonah embolden your evangelism? Pray for those around you who do not know the salvation of Jesus Christ. God hears you.

___
___
___
___
___

"God has the beautiful ability to take the worst things ever and turn them into the best things ever."

STREET LEVEL TRUTH ::

God accomplishes his unshakable, unstoppable plan through the valid choices of people like you and me. He is awesome in power and tender in heart. He hears your prayers and responds to your cries.

PRAYER ::

Lord, I am amazed that you hear my prayers and respond to me with grace. When I hear your hard words, may I remember behind those words is a tender-hearted redeemer. May I understand that I am being loved. Give me the strength to run to you in those moments. In Jesus' name, amen.

MEMORY VERSE ::

Psalm 86:5 (ESV)

For you, O Lord, are good and forgiving, abounding in steadfast love to all who call upon you.

SEVEN

Do you want what God wants?

Are you angry with God? If we were honest with ourselves, many of us would have to answer that we are. God does not always do things the way we would like. He doesn't put us in easy situations or around easy people. But God has not let us down. God has put us in places where His grace can shine through us. God has put you where you are in order to make invisible grace visible.

> It displeased Jonah exceedingly, and he was angry. And he prayed to the LORD and said, "O LORD, is not this what I said when I was yet in my country? That is why I made haste to flee to Tarshish; for I knew that you are a gracious God and merciful, slow to anger and abounding in steadfast love, and relenting from disaster. Therefore now, O LORD, please take my life from me, for it is better for me to die than to live."
>
> And the LORD said, "Do you do well to be angry?"
> **Jonah 4:1-4 (ESV)**

1) Is there any area of your life where you are disappointed with God? Take some time to examine your heart.

_____
_____
_____
_____
_____

2) Is there anyone in your life that you view as a hassle or an irritation? According to the video, why has God put you in his or her life? Does this change the way you view your relationship with that person?

___

"God makes his invisible grace visible by sending people of grace to give grace to people who need grace."

___

3) We tend to love grace until we have to give it to the people around us. What has God redeemed you from in the past? What is God currently redeeming you from?

"You know that you are in deep spiritual trouble when the sin of others concerns you more than your own."

4) We share an identity with lost people because we are sinners. How do you respond to people who disagree with you at work? At home? Do you share law and condemnation or grace and forgiveness?

_____
_____
_____
_____
_____
_____

5) Who are the people God has put into your life as witnesses of grace? Be specific. How can you show them that you love them this week?

_____
_____
_____
_____
_____
_____

"If your eyes ever see or your ears ever hear the sin, weakness, or failure of another person, it's never an accident, it's never an interruption, it's never a hassle—it's always grace."

STREET LEVEL TRUTH ::

We are not on the same page as God when we desire to share law and condemnation with the people around us. Christians are to be a people of grace, who seek to share that grace with everyone around them.

PRAYER ::

Lord, thank you for using an ancient prophet to reveal my heart. God, I confess that I do not always have your heart. I do not love others as you have loved me. Help me to look for those places where I'm disappointed with you. I pray that those moments would create a greater understanding of your grace so that I would rush to you instead of running from you. In Jesus' name, amen.

MEMORY VERSE ::

1 John 4:19-20 (ESV)

We love because he first loved us. If anyone says, "I love God," and hates his brother, he is a liar; for he who does not love his brother whom he has seen cannot love God whom he has not seen.

EIGHT

What does it mean to follow God?

The last section of Jonah exposes a heart problem both in the prophet and in us. We worship created things over the creator and, like young children, become angry when God graciously takes them from us. God patiently points out our sins, not to anger us, but because he is kind and full of grace. He puts us in difficult situations so that we might see and have his heart.

> Jonah went out of the city and sat to the east of the city and made a booth for himself there. He sat under it in the shade, till he should see what would become of the city. Now the LORD God appointed a plant and made it come up over Jonah, that it might be a shade over his head, to save him from his discomfort. So Jonah was exceedingly glad because of the plant. But when dawn came up the next day, God appointed a worm that attacked the plant, so that it withered. When the sun rose, God appointed a scorching east wind, and the sun beat down on the head of Jonah so that he was faint. And he asked that he might die and said, "It is better for me to die than to live." But God said to Jonah, "Do you do well to be angry for the plant?" And he said, "Yes, I do well to be angry, angry enough to die." And the LORD said, "You pity the plant, for which you did not labor, nor did you make it grow, which came into being in a night and perished in a night. And should not I pity Nineveh, that great city, in which there are more than 120,000 persons who do not know their right hand from their left, and also much cattle?   Jonah 4:5-11 (ESV)

"God in patient love is still harnessing the forces of nature for the sole purpose of getting at the heart of one single man."

1) God sent a whale for Jonah in chapter one and now sends a worm. Do you believe God is in sovereign control of every living thing? What is your view of the cosmos?

___

2) God is in control and he is a God of grace. Even so, we frequently choose our own desires over his. Are you like Jonah? Are you more concerned with your own kingdom and comfort than God's kingdom?

___

"Idolatry is not just the desire for evil things; idolatry is about being ruled by good things. A desire for even a good thing becomes a bad thing when it becomes a ruling thing."

3) What is it that makes a good day so good for you? What is it that makes a bad day so bad? What does that tell you about your values and desires?

4) How are your values different than God's? Is there anything you worship before God? Be specific.

"As you recognize how screwed up your values are, you don't have to run from him; you can run to him."

5) Do you have the heart of God? Where do you need to grow? In what areas of your life are you still running from God?

STREET LEVEL TRUTH ::

God is patient, kind, and gentle with us. He shows grace to sinners by forgiving us and by pointing out the areas in our lives where we still run from him to worship idols.

PRAYER ::

God, thank you for Jonah. Thank you for using him to expose my own sin and waywardness. I confess that I still run from you and become angry when you smash my idols. I pray that I may turn to your grace so that I might love what you love, value what you value, and forgive as you forgive. In Jesus' name, amen.

MEMORY VERSE ::

1 Peter 2:24 (ESV)

He himself bore our sins in his body on the tree, that we might die to sin and live to righteousness. By his wounds you have been healed.

THOUGHTS ::

THOUGHTS ::

Get the series that started it all and still challenges us today.

Trek through the book of Philippians with Matt Chandler.

THE HUB

www.gotothehub.com

WANT VIDEO
BIBLE STUDY SERIES
FROM CHRISTIAN LEADERS
YOU TRUST?

www.gotothehub.com

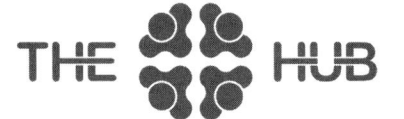

THE HUB

THE MINGLING OF SOULS

MARRIAGE & DATING CONFERENCE

MATT AND LAUREN CHANDLER

+ON DEMAND for your small groups or church

MINGLINGOFSOULS.COM

WANT A BIBLE STUDY TO SUIT YOUR INTERESTS?

WE'VE GOT A SERIES FOR THAT.

www.gotothehub.com

THE HUB

Apologetics	 Bible History & Culture	 Books of the Bible	 Children	 Christian Life
 Christmas & Easter	 Culture	 Theology	 Marriage & Parenting	 Men's Ministry
 Relationships	 Small Group Resources	 Spiritual Growth	 Students and Teens	 Women's Ministry